# 3D PEN
# TEMPLATES

## 50
### 3D PEN STENCILS FOR BOYS & GIRLS

# Introduction

In this booklet, you will discover a fascinating world in which your creativity knows no bounds. With the 3D pens, you can create incredible works of art and bring your own ideas into the third dimension. There is so much to learn when working with 3D pens!

When holding the pen and drawing in the air, you train your dexterity and your spatial imagination. You can also bring your imagination to life with 3D pens. You can create figures, animals, buildings and so much more.

Let's dive into the world of 3D pens and find out what you can do with them and how they work. Get ready to unleash your creativity and join us on an exciting adventure! The possibilities are endless.

# Content

# 1. Basics

**What can you do with 3D pens?**

With 3D pens, you can let your imagination run wild and create a variety of things.

- You can bring figures and toys to life. Create your own action heroes, animals or fantasy creatures. Let them come to life in your hands and immerse yourself in a world full of adventure.
Design jewelry and accessories. Create unique bracelets, pendants or hair accessories.
- Let your creativity sparkle and add a personal touch to your style. Decorate your home. Use 3D pens to create individual decorative items. Design vases, picture frames or even small pieces of furniture to embellish your room.
- Repair and modify objects. You can repair broken parts of toys or add new details to them. Give your old items a new coat of paint and make them look like new again.

**How do 3D pens work?**

3D pens may look like conventional pens, but the way they work is completely different. Plastic or a similar material, known as filament, is used in the tip of the pen. The pen heats the filament and melts it so that it becomes liquid.

When you use the 3D pen, you can apply the melted filament to a surface. The filament cools in the air and hardens. This allows you to build up layer by layer and create your three-dimensional creations.

Some 3D pens have buttons that allow you to control the temperature and speed of the filament flow. This allows you to work precisely and achieve different effects.

## Which filaments are available?

There are a variety of filaments that you can use for your 3D pens. Here are the two most common ones:

- **PLA** (polylactide): This filament is environmentally friendly and is made from natural resources such as corn starch or sugar beet. It is easy to handle and hardens quickly.
- **ABS** (acrylonitrile butadiene styrene): ABS filament is robust and resistant. It is well suited for larger projects and can also withstand heavy loads.

When purchasing, make sure that the filament is compatible with your 3D pen.

## Which documents can be used?

You can use different surfaces to draw with your 3D pen. Here are some options:

- **Transparent sleeves** are transparent and smooth. You can place your templates underneath and draw directly on the film. This allows you to follow the contours and achieve precise results.

- **Silicone underlays** are flexible and heat-resistant. They provide a smooth surface for painting and allow you to easily remove your creations once they have hardened.

# 2. Safety & Health

When working with 3D pens, it is important to pay attention to some safety and health aspects in order to avoid unpleasant situations.

Here are some tips:
- Use the 3D pen under adult supervision, especially if you are younger.
- Be careful not to burn yourself on the hot filament. Never touch the tip of the pen while it is in operation and use finger protectors or heat protection gloves if necessary.
- Make sure you are working in a well-ventilated area, as some filaments can give off a slight odor when heated.
- Make sure that the filament is not knotted or tangled during use to avoid unexpected interruptions.
- Keep the 3D pen out of the reach of small children and make sure they do not use it unsupervised.

With these simple safety tips, you can make your 3D pen experience safe and enjoyable.

# 3. Tips & Tricks

When painting with a 3D pen, you can use a few tips and tricks to improve your results and unleash your creativity.

Here are some suggestions:

- Practice on a flat surface first before trying to draw upwards. This will give you a better feel for the pencil and help you to improve your technique.

- You can use the 2D templates in this booklet for these first exercises. Experiment with different temperature settings and filament speeds to find the best flow and consistency for your creations.

- If you want to create complex models, you can use tools such as stencils or pre-made templates to make the construction easier.

- Take the opportunity to make your artwork more interesting by combining different colors or materials. Let your imagination run wild!

- If you make mistakes, don't worry! 3D pens allow you to remove or correct unwanted lines by carefully cutting them off with scissors or a knife.

- Take your time and work in small sections. This allows you to work precisely and add small details.

- Clean the tip of the 3D pen regularly to prevent clogging. Follow the manufacturer's instructions for cleaning and caring for your pen.

These tips will help you improve your skills with the 3D pen and create even more impressive works! Have fun with it!

# 7. Sample instruction

### Step 1 - Preparation

Switch on the 3D pen and heat it to 165-180°C (or the temperature recommended for your filament). to the temperature recommended for your filament).
Then insert the filament with your desired color into the 3D pen - for the helicopter we choose the color yellow.

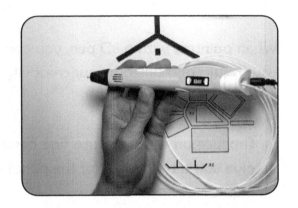

### Schritt 2 - Place carpet pad

Once the 3D pen has been prepared, you can place the carpet pad (e.g. transparent film) over the components of the helicopter that you want to draw first.

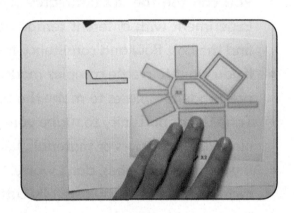

### Step 3 - Draw first components

Use the 3D pen to trace the outline of the individual components on the base and then fill in the shapes. then fill in the shapes.
Pay attention to the number of components, some components have to be drawn several times. Allow the filament to cool on the base and then remove the components from the base.

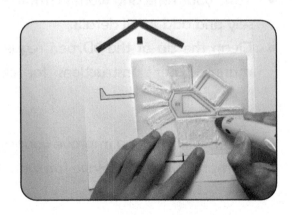

### Step 4 - Connecting components

Then hold two components together and connect them with a 3D pencil line along the edge. Repeat this process for the other yellow components.

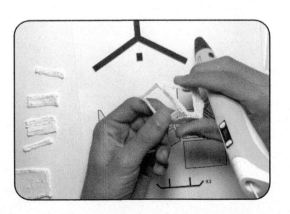

## Step 5 - Change filament
Remove the yellow filament from the 3D pen and insert the black filament.
Before tracing the black parts, press and hold the forward button on the 3D pen until the yellow filament has been completely replaced by the black filament.

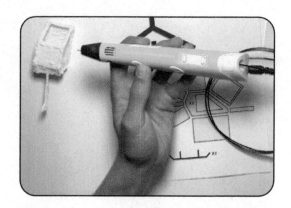

## Step 6 - Draw black elements
Draw the black components of the helicopter
* rotor,
* square connecting piece,
* landing gear,
with the help of the base.

## Step 7 - Assembling the rotor
Attach the square connecting piece to the rotor with a blob of melted filament from the 3D pen. Then attach the rotor with the connecting piece to the roof of the helicopter.

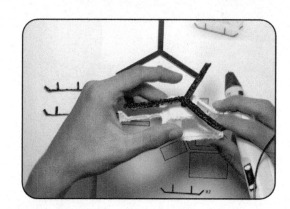

## Step 8 - Final Assembling
Finally, attach the landing gear to the helicopter using a blob of the melted filament. And your 3D pen helicopter is ready.

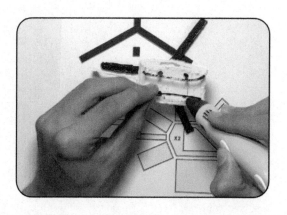

# 2D-Templates

13

# Butterfly

14

# Leafs

# Rainbow

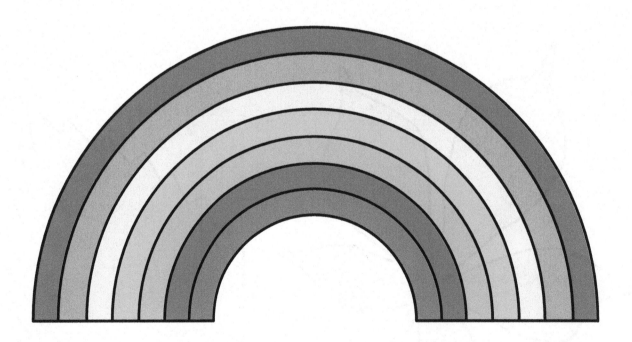

# Heart

# Mask

# Snowflake

# Tennis racket

# Christmas

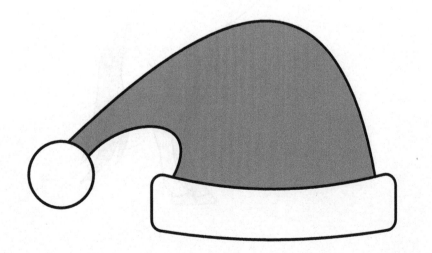

# Unicorn

# Lama

# Cupcakes

Fresh from the bakery.

Decorate the cupcakes with some sprinkles.

# Ice cream

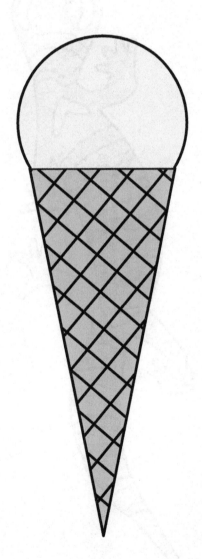

Ohh... a delicious ice cream.

Do you want to add more scoops of ice cream?

# Gecko

# T-Rex

# Ladybug

# Astronaut

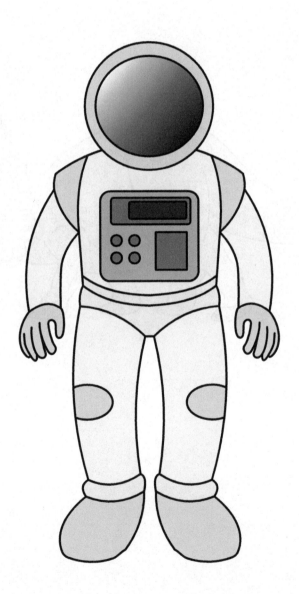

# Triceratops

# Clownfish

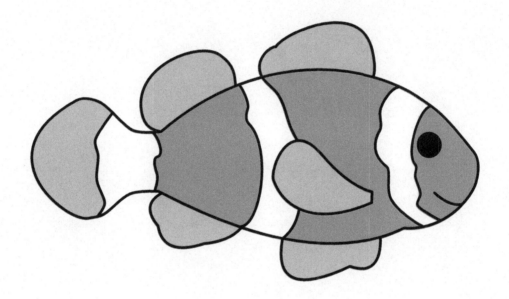

# 3D-Templates

# Umbrella

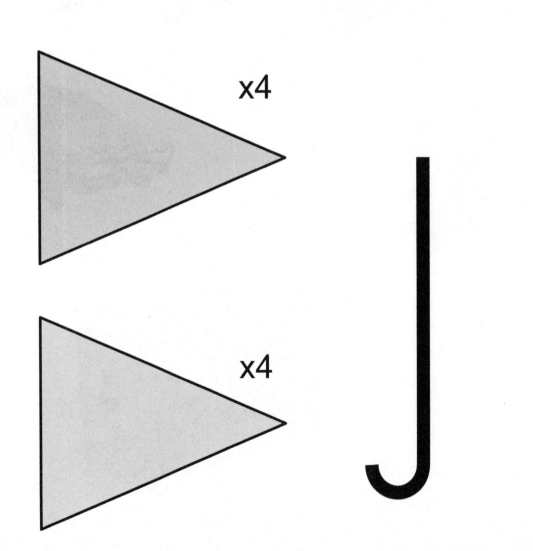

x4

x4

# Plant

# Giraffe

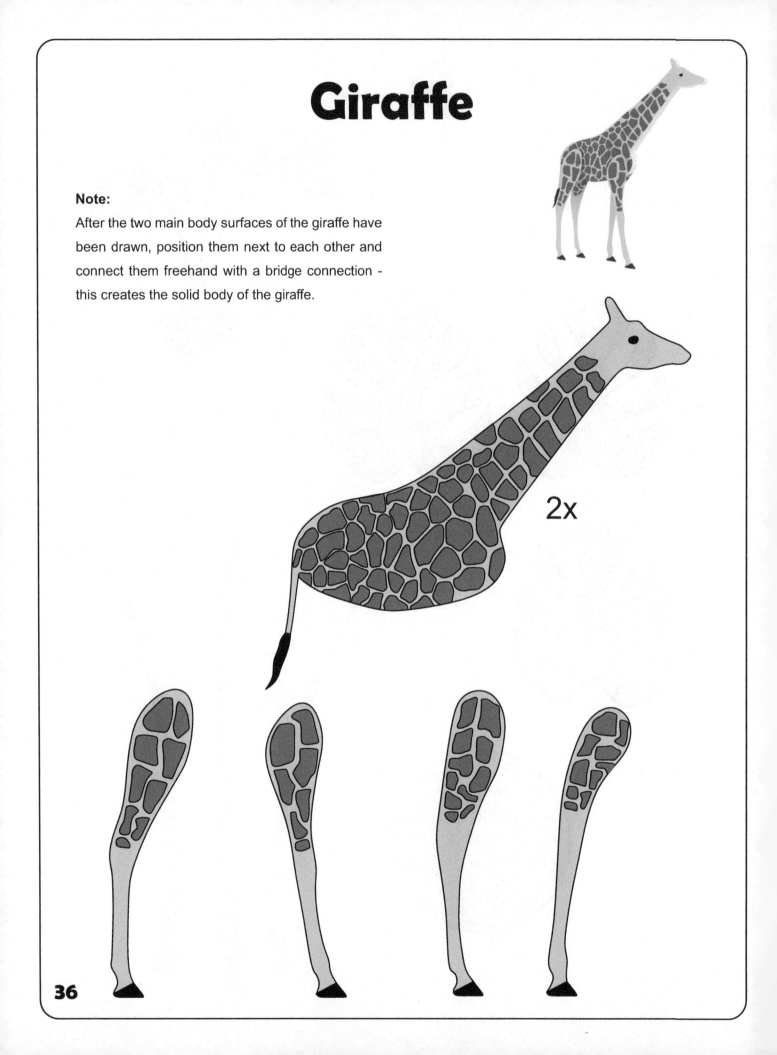

**Note:**

After the two main body surfaces of the giraffe have been drawn, position them next to each other and connect them freehand with a bridge connection - this creates the solid body of the giraffe.

2x

# Heart glasses

# Guitar

**Note:**

After the two main body surfaces of the guitar have been drawn, position them next to each other and connect them freehand with a bridge connection - this creates the solid body of the guitar.

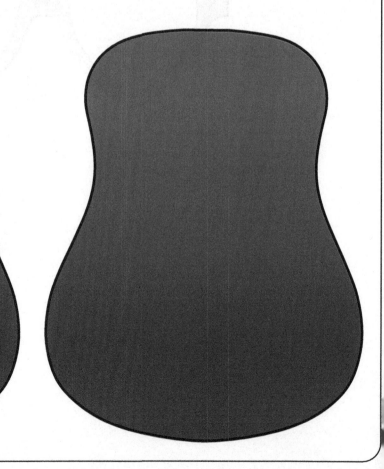

# Golden Gate Bridge

x2

x4

# sunflower

# Couch

# Pine

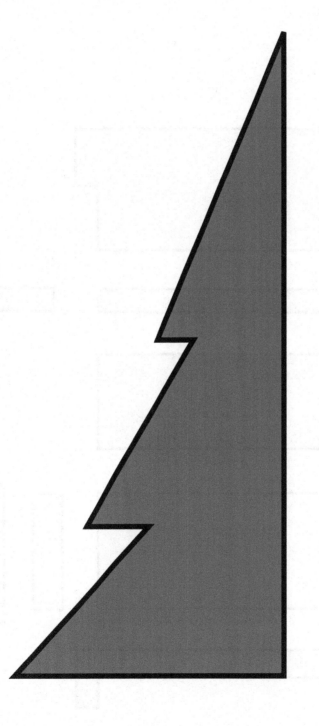

x3

# Rocket

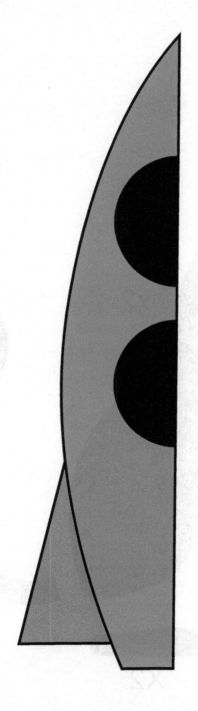

x3

# Cat

**Note:**

After the two main body surfaces of the cat have been drawn, position them next to each other and connect them freehand with a bridge connection - this creates the solid body of the cat.

x2

X2

X2

# Elefant

**Note:**

After the two main body surfaces of the elefant have been drawn, position them next to each other and connect them freehand with a bridge connection - this creates the solid body of the elefant.

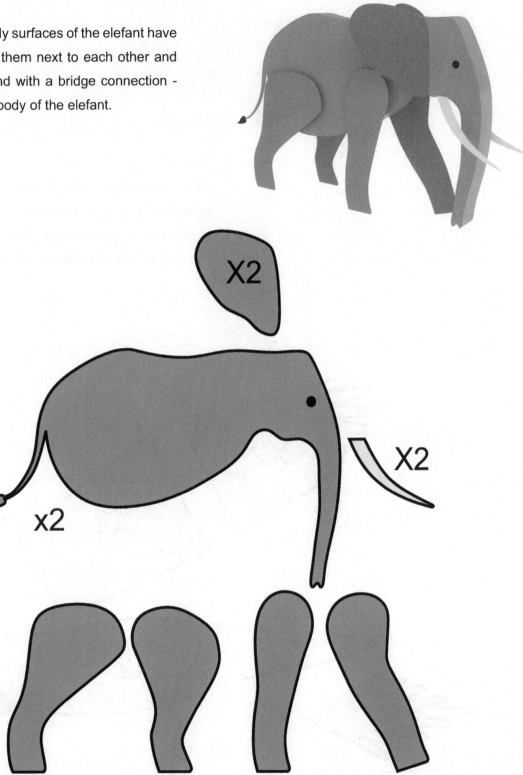

X2

x2

X2

# Parrot

**Note:**

After the two main body surfaces of the parrot have been drawn, position them next to each other and connect them freehand with a bridge connection - this creates the solid body of the parrot.

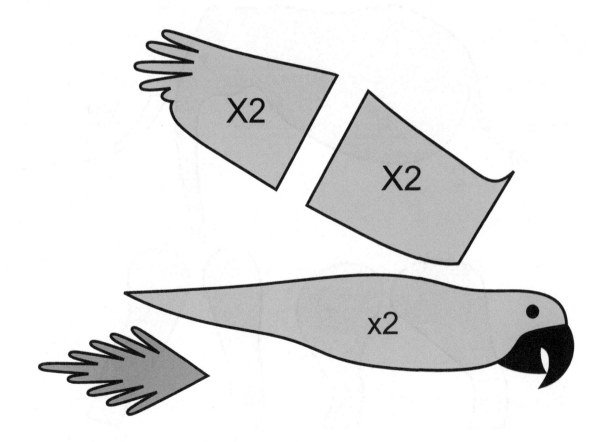

# School bus

X4

47

# Scorpion

**Note:**

After the two main body surfaces of the scorpion have been drawn, position them next to each other and connect them freehand with a bridge connection - this creates the solid body of the scorpion.

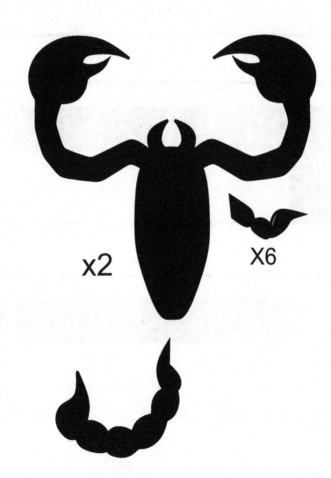

x2          X6

# Windmill

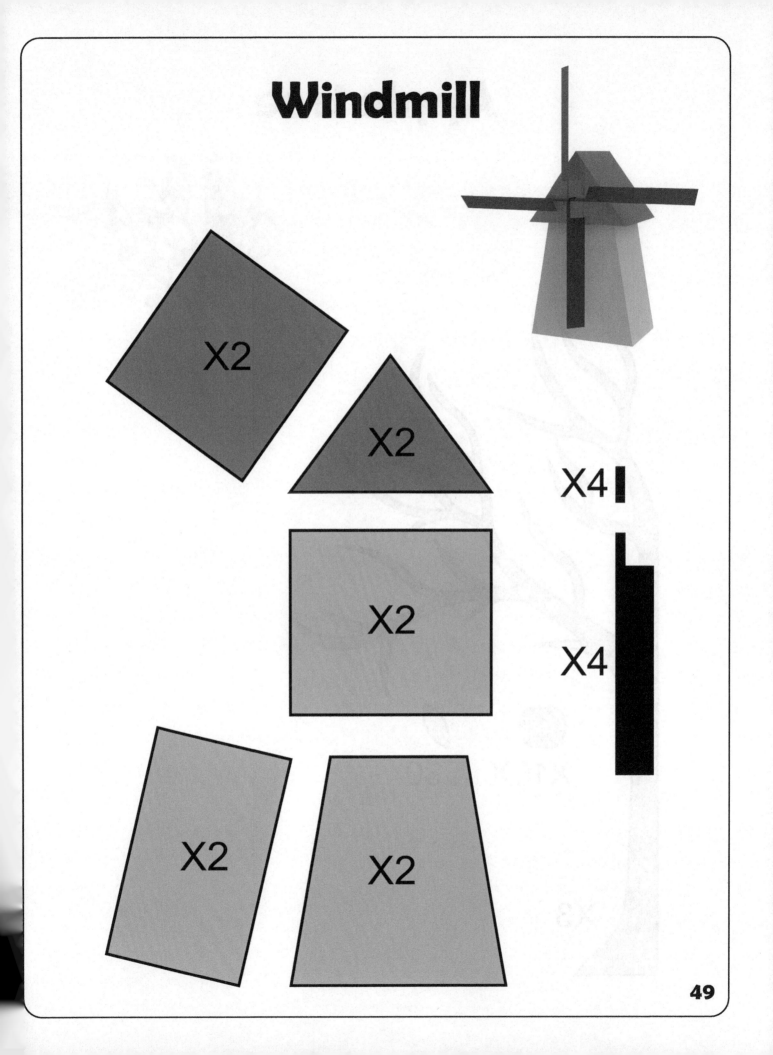

X2

X2

X2

X4

X4

X2

X2

# Apple tree

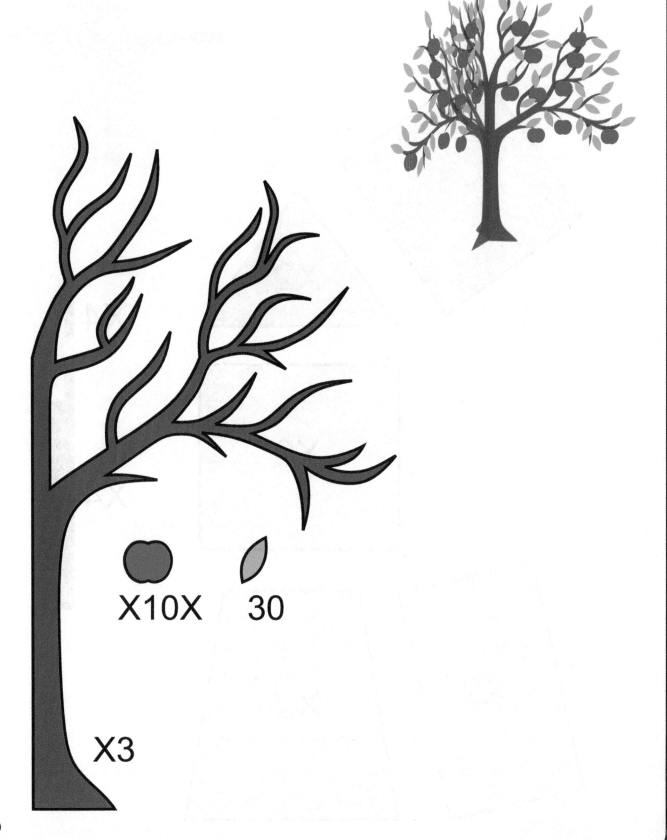

X10X  30

X3

# Excavator

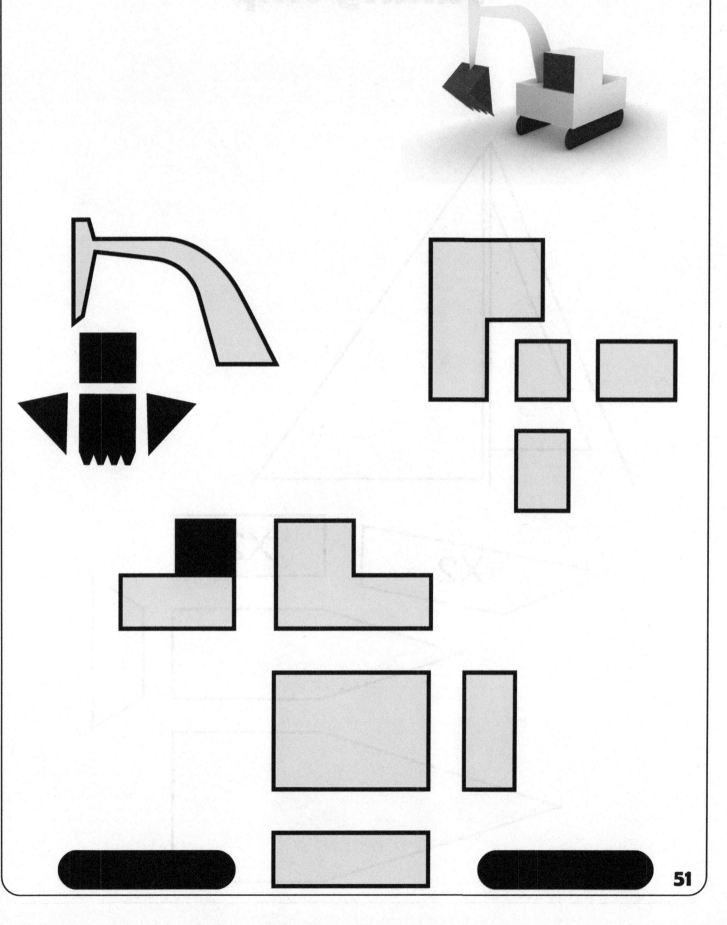

# Sailing ship

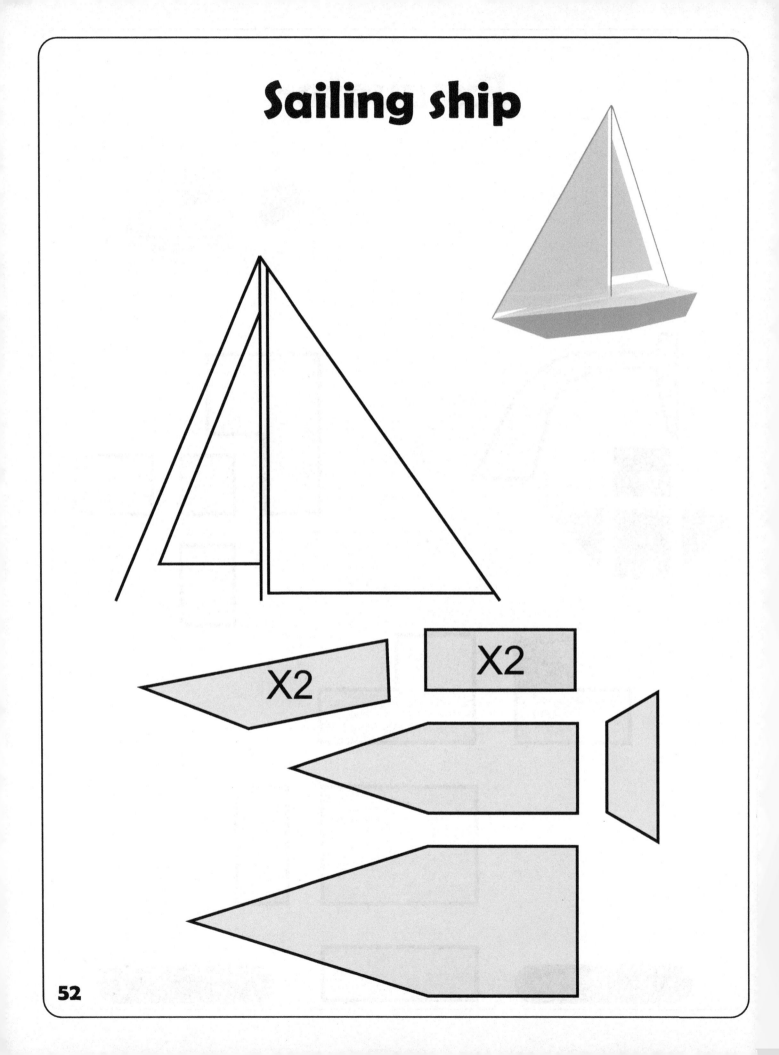

X2

X2

# Biplane

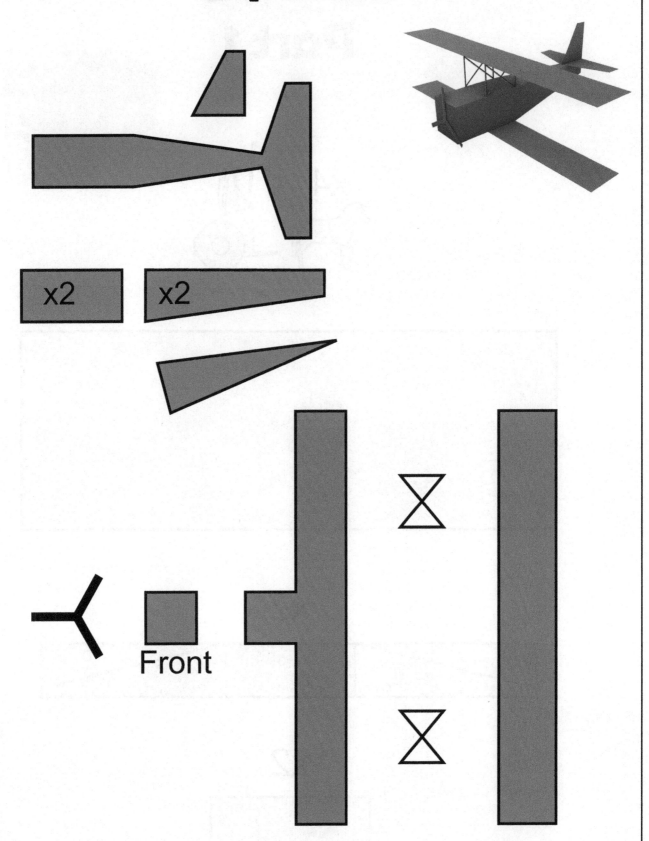

x2

x2

Front

# Brandenburg Gate
## Part 1

x4

x2

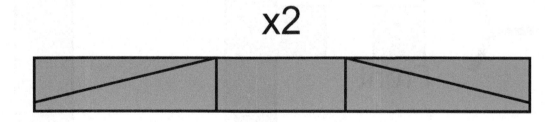

x2

# Brandenburg Gate
## Part 2

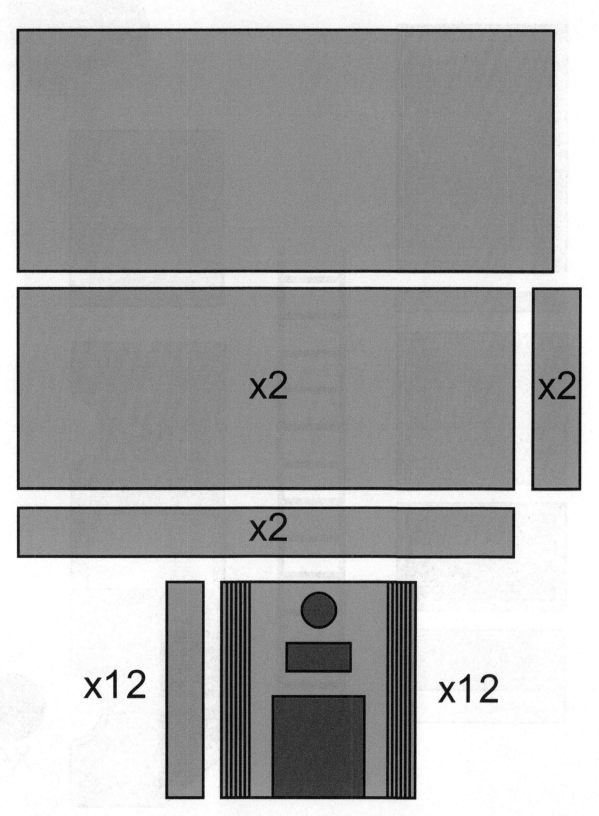

# Fire department car

x2

x4

# Robot

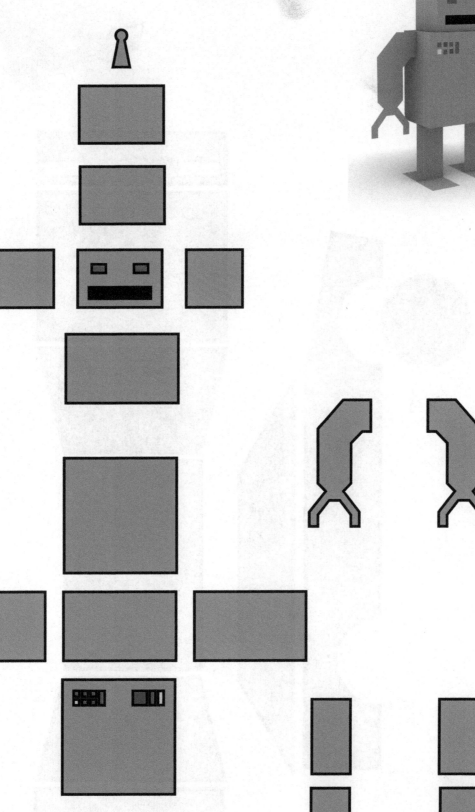

# Car

x4

x2

x2

# Bike

# Tractor

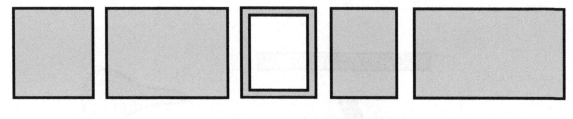

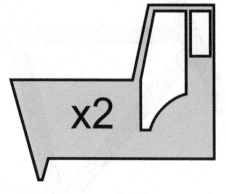

x2

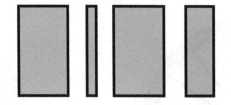

# Ring

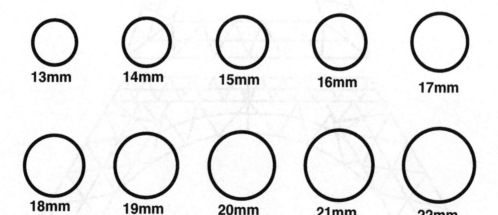

13mm 14mm 15mm 16mm 17mm

18mm 19mm 20mm 21mm 22mm

# Eiffel Tower

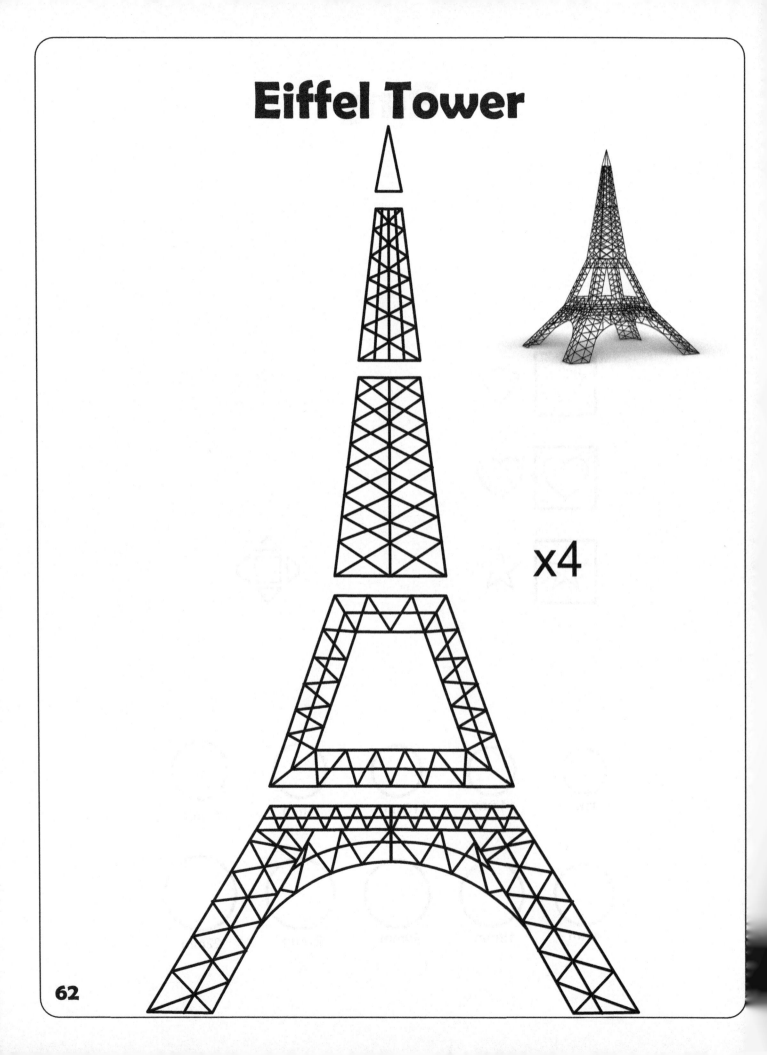

x4

# Camera

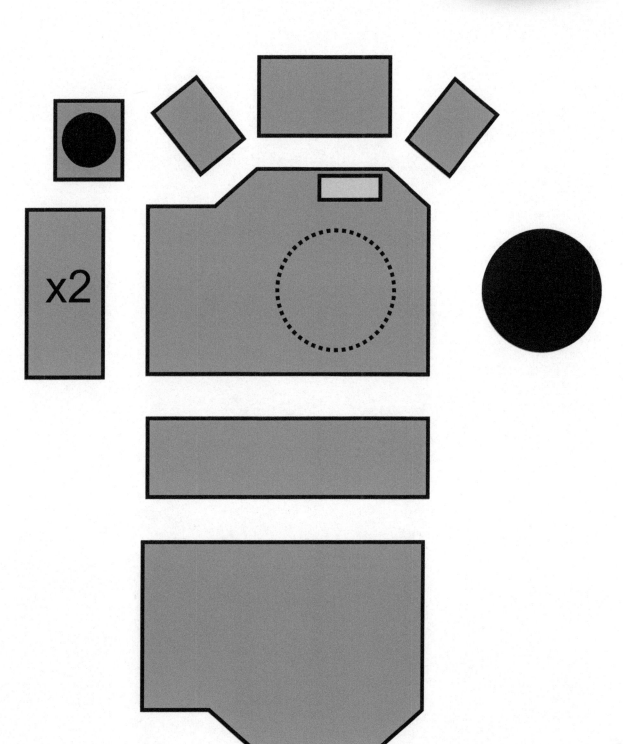

# Rocking chair

# Shark

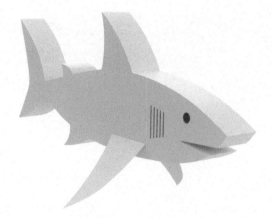

**Please note:**

After the two main body surfaces have been drawn,
position them next to each other and connect them
freehand with a bridge connection - this creates the
solid body of the shark.

X2

# House

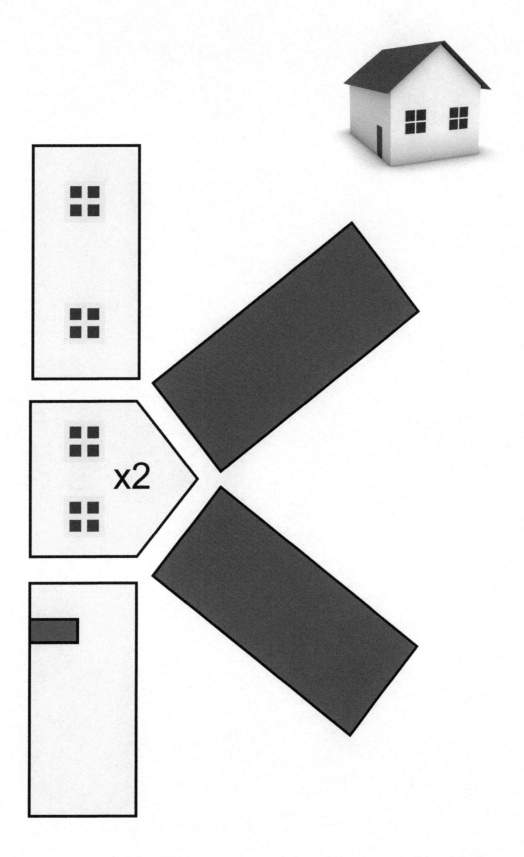

# 6. Contact

If you have any feedback on this magazine or questions please send us an e-mail:

hallo@buchfreund.org

We will take care of your request as soon as possible. Thank you very much.

If you are satisfied with this booklet for 3D pen templates, we look forward to a review on Amazon.

**Impressum**

Christian Kühn
Wiederitzscher Straße 6
04155 Leipzig
Germany